9 STEP GUIDELINE TO SECURING 100K+ IN FUNDING

Learn To Secure Your Financial Situation

DEFONTE WILLIAMS

STEP 1

PROPER BUSINESS STRUCTURE

- Get Your Business Email (*Godaddy.com*)
- Get Your Business Address (*regus.com*)
- Get Your Business Phone Number (*Kall8.com*)
- Get on (*Listyourself.com*) get your business in public records
- Get Your LLC (Sectary of state website) (Keep business name general (Last name solutions LLC or last name Enterprises LLC)
- Get your EIN Number FREE (*irs.gov*)

Have to set this up properly. It's important with the banks.

STEP 2

MAKE YOUR LLC A FOREGIN ENTITY
(TO GET FUNDING IN ALL 50 STATES)
(WHAT MOST PEOPLE MISS OUT ON)
FOREIGN ENTITY EXPLAINED:

Some banks are geographically dependent, and they require you to live or do business within a certain area & they'll ask for your zip-code to screen you.

One way to get around that is to do a foreign Entity! You take your LLC that's already established and register it in another state in which you wish to get funding. Get a Virtual Address to go with it , and then apply for that BUSINESS CREDIT CARD , Loan, LINES OF CREDIT OR ALL 3 from one bank !.

HOW TO GET THE HIGHEST LIMITS POSSIBLE — (Go into bank meet a rep build a relationship with them get them to let you go directly through them for your business credit card applications with rep) Only way to get 40k/50/60k/75k limits on one card!

STEP 3

BUILD YOUR CREDIT REPORT
HOW THE BANKS WANTS YOU TO BULID IT
(CREDIT PROFILE BLUEPRINT)
(GET A HIGH LIMIT ON THE PERSONAL SIDE GETSBETTER HIGHER LIMIT APPROVAL ODDS)

What a fundable credit report should consist of:

- 10% or less of credit utilization
- 100% on time payment history
- 0 Derogatory marks
- 4 Years Or More Of Credit History

- 12 Accounts Positive Accounts
- 2 Or No Hard Inquiries In Each Bureau

STEP 4

TOP 15 BANKS LIST THATS JUST AS GOOD OR BETTER THEN NAVY FEDERAL

- Banner Federal Credit Union
- Truist (0% Interest Cards) (3 no doc Producers 1 inquiry)
- (EQ PULL)
- PSECU (3 no doc products 1 inquiry) (EX PULL)
- Franklin Mint Fed Credit Union
- NASA
- CADENCE (EX PULL)
- M&T
- Envisiion Bank (Transunion)
- UMPQUA
- USAA
- Key Bank (0% Interest Cards)
- Chase Business ink (0% Interest Cards) (EX & TU PULL)
- Alliant
- First Tech
- FDU
- FNBO (EX PULL)
- PENFED (EQU PULl)

STEP 5

BUSINESS FUNDING 50K-300K QUALIFICATIONS!

- 700 CREDIT SCORE or HIGHER
- LEAST 2 CREDIT CARDS THAT BEEN OPEN FOR 1 YEAR
- NO COLLECTIONS
- NO CHARGE OFFS
- NO LATE PAYMENTS
- NO BANKRUPTCY
- UTILIZATION UNDER 15%
- 2-3 INQUIRIES OR LESS IN EACH BUEARU
- LEAST 4 YEARS OF AGE HISTORY
- HAVE TO MEET ALL REQUIREMENTS Small business line of credit

IF Your Business been open for 2 years:

- Wells Fargo - up to 100k no docs online - PG
- US bank - Up to 50k no docs online NO PG
- Key Bank - Up to 50k no docs in branch PG
- Huntington bank- Up to 50k no docs In branch PG
- Fundbox up to 150k no docs online NO PG
- Bluevine line of credit Up to $250,000 6 months in
- business 600* Fico score make 10k/ mth for 6 months

STEP 6

FUNDING SEQUENCES PERSONAL CREDIT & BUSINESS CREDIT

Know Exactly what banks pull from which buearu so we can apply strategic with less inquiry (List of what banks I go for)

Personal Funding Sequence

Experian: PSECU (CC & LOC 20k!) Chase (2) Citi, First Tech CC & LOC, Amex (2) = 7 accounts (4 inquiries) Discover (5k-15k)

Transunion: BOA (2), APPLE (0), NAVY FCU (1), Light Stream (1) = 5 accounts (5 inquiries)

Equifax: DCU (1) NIHFCU (3) PENFED (2) SECU of MD (3)

Should be able to accumilate 150k +

BUSINESS FUNDING

- Experian
    - Paypal Business Credit card
    - Chase Business Ink (Best to have inside rep run application)
    - First Tech: Put Income (73k) Odyssey Rewards World Elite MasterCard. Get 4 CRedit Cards 1 inquiries /Amex charge (Open 4 Different internet browsers (safari, Firefox, crome, internet explore) (fill out all applications til 98% filled Out) (apply for all of them at once!)
    - Fnbo
    - Captal on Tap
    - Paypal Business Credit card
    - Original Platinum Amex charge card
    - Original Gold Delta
    - Gold Delta platinum
    - Plum Business Plum
    - Fnbo
    - Pnc
    - Oak Vally Community Bank
    - Cadence bank

- Equifax
    - Elan powered card Flagstar bank
    - Banner iCU
    - US bank
    - Comerica bank
    - First financial northwest bank

- Transunion
    - PayPay Businesss Credit card
    - Barclays jet blue
    - Navy
    - Ameris Bank

(Inquiry Sensitive) Light Stream First- Apply for used auto loan for 20k if you never had an auto loan or small loan (Income) 73k Check stubs are sometimes required Apply for more than 20k if you had a decent auto loan already reported (Inquiry Sensitive) Alliant open an account with them For $5 the for a credit card (Income) 73k Visa Platinum Rewards as low as 0% introductory rate

Fidelity- Open brokerage account with them first then apply for credit card the same day They have beeb giving away high limits for 12 months on purchases and balance transfers (After the introductory period a low standard variable rate applies ranging from 13.24% to 23.24% Balance transfer fee of 2% of the transferred $5 minimum)

- Earn 5,000 bonus points with qualified spending
- Earn two rewards points for every dollar spent Amazing Credit Line Works with at mobile forms of payment.
- Apple, Google and Samsung Pay
- No Annual Fee

Flagstar Bank- This is an Elan powered bank credit card that issues high limits I recommend Elan powered cards because they give 0% introductory Up to 12 to 20 months (Visa Signature Max Cash Preferred Card

STEP 7

BUSINESS CREDIT CARD STACKING METHOD! (PG METHOD)

Once your credit profile is funding qualified like I showed in the book earlier (We are going to Personal Guarantee Each Card)

(Don't be scared to PG and have them pull your personal it's still going to be separate! Just be smart with the Money)

Then we can go to multiple banks back to back to back.

- Ex; Go to chase get a business credit card 10K-20k+
- Then go to Bank of America apply for business credit card
- Then go to PNC Apply for business credit card
- Then go to Tusit Apply for business credit card
- And go to 10 Banks! And Stack your business credit cards

so, once you go to all of those banks then you will accumulate 6 figures in credit.

Yes, they will give you hard inquires BUT they are not attached to open accounts so we can remove inquires and repeat the process!!

STEP 8

HOW I FILL OUT THE APPLICATIONS!

(*Business Income* - $375,000/ Personal $180,000 / (75k For Amex, Nih Fcu money in the market $250,000 / money saved $220,500....... Industry: Profession Scientific and Technical > other professional> all other professionals or Marketing and advertising helping businesss grow online.

Rent or mortgage: only half of my full amount. How long at address: At least 2 years or more Job: Always employed for self if you do not have job. At least 2 years on the job. Checking and Savings Account: Always both

STEP 9

AFTER YOU DO ROUND 1 WE CAN REMOVE INQUIRES BECAUSE THEY NOT ATTACHED TO OPEN ACCOUNTS AND THEY ONLY REPORT TO THE BUSINESS SIDE!
SO, UTILIZATION IS A NON-FACTOR!

EXTRA BONUS PAGE

Multiple cards or lines of credit with 1 inquiry NIHFCU

- PENFED
- BANK OF AMERICA
- US BANK
- SECU OF MD
- CHASE
- AMERICAN EXPRESS
- CAPITAL ONE

EQUIFAX PULLS

- DIGITAL FCU
- NATIONAL RESEARCH LAB FCU
- STATE EMPLOYEE CU OF MD
- NIHFCU SIGNAL FCU
- SKYPOINT FCU
- PENFED JUSTICE FCU
- CHEVRON FCU
- LANGLEY FCU AMERIS BANK OF TEXAS

EQUIFAX PULLS

- NAVY FCU
- APPLE FCU
- LAKE MICHIGAN FCU
- TOWER FCU
- LIGHTSTREAM APPLE CREDIT CARD
- REGIONS BANK
- HUNTINGTON BANK
- FIFTH THIRD BOA BARCLAY

Defonte Williams

Name of Lender / Credit Bureau / Minimum Credit Score Needed (if it's available)

Amex – Experian

Bank of America - Equifax

Barclaycard Apple Rewards – Experian (720+ $3,500)

BMW Financial Services – Experian

BMW Financial Services – Experian (695+ $50,000 Lease)

Capital One Auto Finance – Experian – Equifax

Capital One Auto Finance – Experian (650+ $30,000 with Proof of Income)

Capital One Bank Credit Cards – Equifax – Transunion

Capital One Venture – Experian – Transunion (650+ $5,000)

Capital One Quick Silver 1 – Experian (600+ $500)

Capital One Venture – Experian (680+ $20,000 with 2 AU's over $10,000 each)

Car Smart – Transunion

Carmax – Experian – Equifax – Transunion

CBNA Credit Cards – Experian – Equifax

Centric Credit Union Visa – Experian (530+ $500)

Chase Bank – Experian & Equifax

Chase – Experian (750+ $10,000)

Chase Amazon Rewards – Experian (750+ $7,000)

Chase Freedom – Experian (750+ $7,000)

Chase Ink Bold – Experian (720+ $15,000)

Chase Sapphire Preferred – Experian (720+ $18,000) Chase

Southwest Plus – Experian (750+ $3,500)

Chase Amazon Rewards – Experian (750+ $7,000) Chase

Freedom – Experian (750+ $7,000)

Chase Ink Bold – Experian (720+ $15,000)

Chase Sapphire Preferred – Experian (720+ $18,000) Chase

Southwest Plus – Experian (750+ $3,500)

Chase United Explorer – Experian (720+ $19,500)

Citibank Best Buy - Equifax

Citi American Airlines Platinum – Experian (720+ $6,500)

Citi Double Cash / Citi Thank You Premier – Experian (720+ $6,800)

Citizen's Bank (location specific) Equifax

Community First Credit Union – Equifax (region specific)

Community – Transunion or Equifax

Credit Union of Texas – Equifax

Credco Auto Reseller – Experian – Transunion

Chrysler Credit – Transunion – Does Not Re Report to D&B Dell Computers Preferred Account – Experian (690+ $1,500) Delta Skymiles Gold Amex – Experian (660+ $5,000)

Digital Credit Union DCU Personal Loan – Experian (700+ $26,000)

Digital Credit Union DCU Auto Loan – Experian (700+ $25,000 with Proof of Income)

Direct TV - Equifax

Discover Card – Equifax – Transunion

Discover It – Experian (620+ $1,500 - $5,500)

Drive Finance Auto Financing – Experian – Transunion

Elan Financial - Equifax

Fifth Third Bank – Transunion

FIA Amex Fidelity American Express – Experian (740+ $9,000)

Fidelity Amex Investment Rewards – Experian (720+ $12,500)

Fidelity Investment Rewards Visa Signature Card – Experian (750+ $7,500)

FirstBank Credit (FNBO) SavingStar Amex – Experian (650+ $1,000)

FNBO/NRA – Experian (740+ $8,500)

First Choice Bank – Primer Visa – Experian – Equifax – Transunion First

Data Merchant Services – Credit Card Merchant Account Processor

Greater Texas FCU – Experian (620+ $27,000)

Hertz Corporation – Equifax Home

Depot – Experian (650+) HSBC –

Transunion

Jared/Sterling – Experian (600+ $1,500)

JCB Marukai Premium California – Experian (750+ $5,000 with Proof of Income)

JCrew (Comenity) – Experian (600+ $750)

JP Morgan Chase Business – Transunion – Chexsystems JP Morgan Chase Bank – Equifax

Kohls – Experian (560 $300)

Lexus Financial Services – Experian (690+ $90,000 with Lease)

Mercedes Auto – Transunion + Experian + Equifax

Macys – Experian (700+ $1,000)

NASA FCU Platinum Rewards – Experian

NASA Visa Platinum Cash Rewards – Experian (735+ $20,000)

Navy Federal Credit Union – Equifax – Transunion

NFCU GoRewards Visa – Experian (660+ $1,000)

Navy Federal Credit Union – Business – Transunion

Nordstrom – Experian (620+ $1,000)

OneMain Financial – Equifax

Overstock.com Comenity Bank – Experian (640+ $2,200)

PEX Card – Will Start Experian Business File

PNC Bank – Experian

PNC Bank – Experian (750+ $10,000)

Prosper – Experian (640+ $15,000) RBS –

Citizens Bank – Equifax

Red Check – Equifax

Restoration Hardware – Experian (700+ $2,000) Road Loans – Equifax

Sam's Club -Experian (660+ $700)

SchoolsFirst FCU – Experian (660+ $12,000)

Sprint Nextel –Equifax

Sportsmans Guide Comenity Bank – Experian (680+ $2,500)

SunTrust Bank – Transunion

Stash (Synchrony) - Experian

TD Signature Visa – Experian (700+ $5,000)

Tempur-Pedic – Wells Fargo Financial National Bank – Experian (745+ $5,000)

TD Bank - Experian

T-Mobile – Equifax – Transunion

True Value Comenity Bank – Experian (640 $350)

USAA - Equifax

Verizon Wireless – Equifax – Experian Vystar – Equifax (region specific)

Victoria's Secret – Experian Wells Fargo Bank – Experian – Chexsysems

Wells Fargo Credit Cards – Equifax

Wells Fargo Auto Finance – Experian – Equifax

Affinity Plus (Join Foundation)

Allegacy Federal CU (Join Association application process) Applied Bank

Barclays

BBVA Compass Bank

CFNA

Discover (Equifax 50% of the time)

Eaton Family CU (**Ohio Only**) Fifth Third Bank

First Premier Bank

GECRB (General Electric Capital Retail Bank)

John Deere Financial

KEMBA Financial CU (Angie's List Eligible, used to pull Equifax)

Lake Michigan CU (ALS Assoc Eligible)

Lending Club

Mazuma CU (Join Harry S Truman Library & Museum

Mercedes Benz Credit Corp

Merrick Bank

Michigan First CUPNC (TU 50% of the time)

Regions Bank (region specific)

RBFCU

Smart Financial CU ($60 to join Houston Museum)

Synchrony Bank (See store card listing below held by Synchrony bank). Note synchrony also pulls from Experian

State Farm
UMB
U.S. Bank VW

BRANDS AND STORE CARDS TRANSUNION BASED:

Amazon Store (SYNCHRONY AND CHASE)
American Eagle (SYNCHRONY)
Ameriprise (Barclays)
Apple (Barclays)
Ashley Furniture (SYNCHRONY)
Banana Republic (SYNCHRONY)
Belk (SYNCHRONY)
Babies R Us (SYNCHRONY)
Barclaycard Arrival
BJ's (Barclays)
Bridgestone (CFNA)
Care Credit (SYNCHRONY)
Chevron (SYNCHRONY)
Dillard's (SYNCHRONY) eBay (GECRB)
Firestone (Citibank)
Gap (SYNCHRONY)
Golfsmith (SYNCHRONY)
Guide Dogs (UMB)
H.H.Gregg (SYNCHRONY)
Hooters (Merrick Bank)

JCPenneys (SYNCHRONY)

Old Navy (SYNCHRONY)

PayPal (SYNCHRONY)

Priceline (Barclays)

QVC (SYNCHRONY)

Rooms To Go (SYNCHRONY)

Sallie Mae (Barclays)

Sam's Club (SYNCHRONY)

Texaco (SYNCHRONY) TJX (SYNCHRONY)

Toys R Us (SYNCHRONY)

Travelocity (Barclays)

UPromise (Barclays) US Air (Barclays)

Walmart (SYNCHRONY)

Williams Sonoma (Barclays)

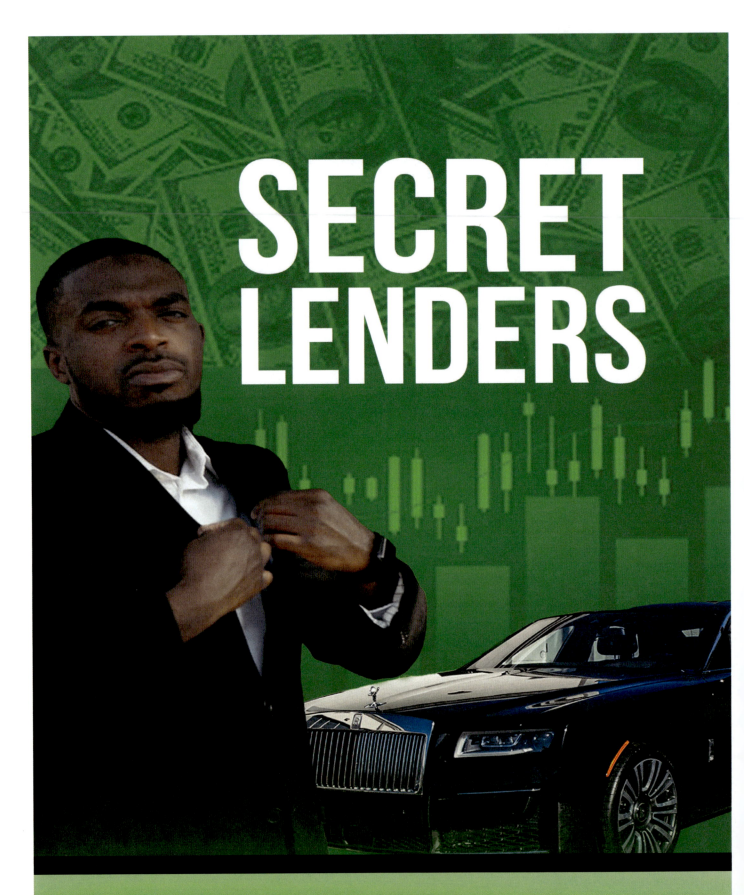

5 Steps
HOW I MADE 6 FIGURES OFF A $37 DIGITAL PRODUCT

Fonte Solutions

CREATE THE EBOOK

- Create the Title.
    - We like to use "5 best steps to do this" or "7 best steps to do that."
    - Make the title brief and to the point! DON'T OVER THINK IT! Just create it.
- Get a 3D cover made on Fiverr.com.
    - Make sure to choose someone with 5 stars and over 100 ratings.
- Write an outline.
    - We use ChatGPT.
- Finish it with your own words and touches, and proofread it.
- Put the file in pdf format; you can even have someone on Fiverr create the pdf with your graphics, colors, and logos.

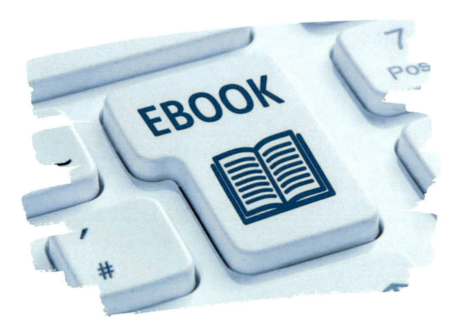

CREATE A PAGE TO SELL YOUR EBOOK ON

- Create a Click Funnels account
- Create a landing page on Click Funnels (or get someone on <u>fiverr.com</u> to create this landing page for you) with a cover for your book and all your logos, graphics, and colors.
- Price it between 17$- 37$.
- Create an order bump for $9 to make more money.
- Using Fiverr, you can hire someone to:
    - Make the funnel and create pages for an up sale for $147 and a down sale for $47 if they don't buy that item.
    - Create a page to direct buyers to a book call if you have a higher ticket item.
    - Set up the automation for your clients to receive it automatically.

Step #3

CREATE UP AND DOWN SALES, AS WELL AS ORDER BUMPS.

- Make selfie videos for these pages, and tell them it's a one-time offer to buy your up sale or down sale.
- These videos can include:
    - An introduction to the audio version of the book.
    - A checklist of available offers.
    - An actual video of you breaking down what's in the book step-by-step.
- You, or the person making your pages, should also set up automations for these products.

Step #4

SET UP MANY CHAT AUTOMATIONS FOR IG & FACEBOOK

- Designate automation for your comments by creating an automated workflow so that when your audience DMs you or comments a word like "bank," it automatically sends them to your funnel to purchase your book.
    - Set it for your DMs and inboxes on every post or reel.
- Schedule automation for when viewers comment certain words on your live videos.
    - Include the word (or words) in your bio as a LinkTree link.

Step #5

MARKET YOUR BOOK FOR MORE SALES

- Use shout-out pages to direct traffic to your landing page and funnel.
- Post 3 times daily on your page and 8 times daily on your story for the next 30 days, no matter what.
    - Using ChatGPT for content ideas, create good videos discussing the book's benefits, how it can help people, or how it helped you.
- Post about your book being on sale at 1 a.m. and 3 a.m. (you can schedule these posts automatically).
- Collaborate with people from various fields by going live with them.
    - Direct potential buyers to the eBook funnel, and give your collaborator a percentage of the book's proceeds from that day.
- Hire an ad team to run ads to your book funnel on Facebook, Instagram, YouTube, and TikTok. Begin with $20 per day and work your way up.

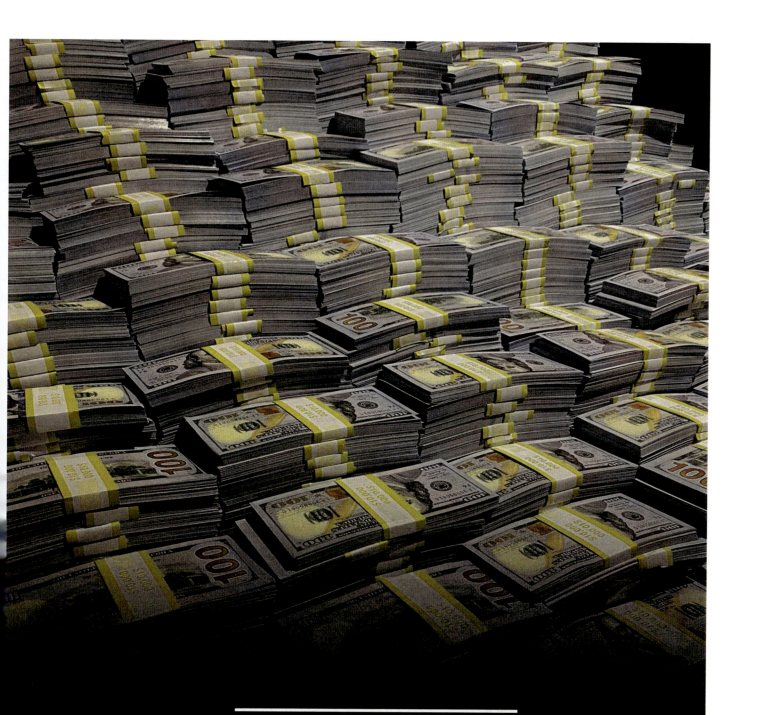

These are the exact strategies we used to make 50,000 in 40 days but over 6 figures in 12 months.

- FB Fonte Williams
- IG fonte_ enterprise
- Tik tok fonte.enterprise

Made in the USA
Middletown, DE
06 December 2024